Then & Now
HORSHAM

In 1951, a relic of the Napoleonic Wars still existed in Armoury Cottages, which formed part of the Depot, built on Horsham Common in 1805. The Depot provided secure accommodation for 10,000 stands of arms, stored here in case Napoleon invaded England through Sussex. Two naval cannon of an earlier date which stood outside the Depot now have a home at Horsham Museum, but Armoury Cottages have disappeared, and new houses have been built in their place.

Then & Now
HORSHAM

COMPILED BY HORSHAM MUSEUM SOCIETY
AND HORSHAM PHOTOGRAPHIC SOCIETY

First published 2001

Tempus Publishing Limited
The Mill, Brimscombe Port,
Stroud, Gloucestershire, GL5 2QG

ISBN 0 7524 2445 9

Typesetting and origination by
Tempus Publishing Limited
Printed in Great Britain by
Midway Colour Print, Wiltshire

This 1951 festival procession, photographed in East Street, was the annual carnival procession which at that time was held on the Thursday evening of Cricket Week – as the long shadows in the photograph indicate. Cricket Week was an important event in the Horsham year at this time – the Sussex team stayed at the Black Horse Hotel and two full county matches were played. The Horsham procession was led by the marching band of Christ's Hospital School, whose pupils, in their distinctive Bluecoat dress, had been a familiar sight in the town for nearly half a century. Christ's Hospital found a new home at Stammerham, just outside Horsham, after it moved out of its original cramped site in London in 1897. The new school, with its railway station, was opened by the Prince of Wales in 1902. Today most of the houses shown in this photograph have disappeared, because it is here that the link road, Park Way, joining Albion Way and East Street has been built.

Contents

Acknowledgements

First of all, our thanks are due to sixteen members of Horsham Photographic Society who created an invaluable record of Horsham in 1951 by taking more than 170 photographs of the town as it was then. They were R. Baldwin, R.E. and W. Batchelor, W. Evans, P. Gilbert, R. Kipps, J.E. Marren, J. Martin, F.G. Mirfield (President), H.C.H. Mumford, A.L. Norman, R. Oulds, D. Streeter, C. Sullivan, C.F. Taylor (Secretary) and W.H. White. C.F. Taylor, who was a dentist by profession, is known to have had the original idea and taken the bulk of the photographs. In the year 2000, seventeen members of the society were involved in retaking the photographs as a Millennium project, namely Les Ansell, Ted Attree, Roger Baker, Chris Clack, Leslie Coates, Marion Coleman, Celia and Ken Cronin, Ray Griffith, Bob Jones, Trudie Mitchell, Ashley Parker, Anne and Chris Phillips, Joyce Smith, Darrell Turner, and Di Wilson. We are especially grateful to Darrell Turner who spent many hours producing a completely new set of prints of the 1951 photographs. Horsham Photographic Society would like to acknowledge support received from Horsham District Council and Royal & Sun Alliance for this project.

We would also like to thank the Curator of Horsham Museum, Jeremy Knight, for making the initial contacts which led to the writing of this book, and for his help and support. In writing the text, Sue Djabri has had the help of members of Horsham Museum Society's Local History Group. David and Pauline Carter, Audrey Goffe, Alicia Hemming, Norman Hewell, Phyl Jackson, Robin Jeffcoate, Maureen Radbourne, Gordon Sharp, Alan Siney, Paul Smith, Sheila Stevens, Brian Sturt, Joan and Terry Tamplin, and Elizabeth Vaughan did research or took part in meetings and reminiscence groups, and provided much useful information and insight. Roger Baker and Darrell Turner contributed some specific information about particular photographs. John Baugh carefully checked the text and made some very constructive suggestions, as did Paul Smith, Terry Tamplin and Elizabeth Vaughan who kindly arranged some of the reminiscence groups and wrote up the notes.

Roger Baker, ARPS, Chairman of Horsham Photographic Society and
Susan C. Djabri, Vice-Chairman (Local History), Horsham Museum Society, 2001

Bibliography

Albery, W., *Reminiscences of Horsham, being the Recollections of Henry Burstow*, (1911); *A Parliamentary History of Horsham*, (1927); and *A Millennium of Facts on the History of Horsham and Sussex*, (1947).

Coomber, G.H.W., *Bygone Corn Mills in the Horsham Area*, (1996); and (with Jean Alexander) *The Horsham Tithe Map Schedule and Index*, (1998).

Djabri, Susan C., *The Horsham Companion*, (1995); and (with A.F. Hughes and J. Knight), *The Shelleys of Field Place*; and *The Letters of Bysshe and Timothy Shelley*, (2000).

Dudley, Howard, *The History and Antiquities of Horsham*, (1836).

Holmes, Frank, *Horsham Town and Country Stories*, (1990).

Horsham and District Official Guides (various); and *Horsham Urban and Rural Directory* 1951-52.

Hudson, T.P. (ed.), *Victoria History of the County of Sussex: Vol. VI, part 2*, (1986).

Hughes, A.F., *Horsham Houses*, (1986); *Causeway Houses*, (1995); and *Seven Horsham Houses*, (1996).
Hurst, Dorothea, *Horsham, its History and Antiquities*, (1868); and second edition, (1886).
Knight, Jeremy, *Horsham, its History 1947-1990*, (1995).
Neale, Kenneth, *Victorian Horsham, The Diary of Henry Michell 1809-1874*, (1975).
Siney, Alan, *The 1840 Tithe Map of Horsham*, (1998).
Wales, Tony, *Horsham in Old Picture Postcards Vol. I*, (1987); and *Vol. II* (1992); *Horsham and District in old Photographs*, (1994); and (with Bill Young); *Horsham Then and Now*, (1999).
Wield, Eileen, *Elizabeth Gatford 1741-1799, Lady of Fortune and Pity*, (1999).
Willson, A.N., *A History of Collyer's School 1532-1964*, (1965).
Windrum, Anthony, *Horsham, an Historical Survey*, (1978); and (with A.F.Hughes), *Bygone Horsham*, (1982).
Yorke, Phillip C., *The Diary of John Baker*, (1931).

Introduction

This book is different from many others in the *Then & Now* series in that the earlier and later photographs span almost exactly fifty years. All the earlier photographs were taken in 1951, and the later photographs in 2000, by members of the Horsham Photographic Society. The idea of producing a detailed pictorial record of the town in 1951 was conceived by the then Secretary, C.F. Taylor. He wanted Horsham residents of 'fifty years hence and beyond' to be able to see what the town was like then. This shows extraordinary prescience in view of the sweeping changes which have taken place in the town during the last half century. Tribute was paid to Taylor's 'magnificent' work by the Chairman of Horsham Urban District Council, Frank G. Holmes, and the President of Horsham Photographic Society, F.G. Mirfield, when the album of photographs was handed over to the Council in March 1952. Fifty years later, current members of the Photographic Society retook the photographs, from exactly the same viewpoint wherever possible, to mark the Millennium and illustrate the changes that have taken place. Four albums containing the two sets of pictures were presented to Horsham District Council by the present Chairman of the Horsham Photographic Society, Roger Baker ARPS, on 23 January 2001, to be kept in the archives of Horsham Museum.

It was at this point that the Local History Group of Horsham Museum Society was asked to provide the text to accompany the pictures chosen for this book. Members of the group have studied the two complete sets of photographs, and those who lived here then here noted down their own memories of Horsham as it was fifty years ago. But in writing this book we have also used many other sources to draw out some significant aspects of the long history of the town, and mention a few of the people who shaped its development.

Horsham is known to have existed for more than one thousand years, and there is now some evidence to suggest that people lived here during the time of the Roman occupation of Britain. The town came into being because it was at a point where a road crossed a river, and communications played an important part throughout its history. It was possible to ford the River Arun easily at this point, and there was enough of a clearing in the great forest, which originally covered the whole of the Sussex Weald, for people to settle and start to cultivate the land. Horsham lies in a hollow, sheltered by low hills, near the source of the River Arun in St Leonard's Forest, so water, fuel and timber for building were all available. After the Romans left Britain at the beginning of the fifth century, Saxons settled in much of southern England, introducing manors and parishes as the basis of their system of local administration. Many of the Saxon manors in the Sussex Downs held land in the Weald, where animals were pastured in the summer. The town is believed to have got the name *'Horse-ham'* which means 'place of horses', because its early settlers gained a reputation as horse breeders.

The first known reference to Horsham is in a charter by which King Eadred granted the manor of Washington, now a small village near Steyning, to his 'very faithful thegn' Eadric, in 947 – Horsham was at this time an outlying part of this manor. William Albery called this charter the town's 'birth certificate'. After the Norman invasion of 1066, it was of great importance for the new rulers to maintain their lines of communication to Normandy, which passed through Sussex. Horsham, by then a manor in its own right, became one of the main points of fortification in the Rape of Bramber, with a motte and bailey north of the town. It was governed by William de Braose, a trusted lieutenant of William the Conqueror. His descendants allowed the townspeople to rebuild the church, in 1231, and to have a July Fair, established by Royal Charter in 1233. This suggests that Horsham already functioned as a market town for the surrounding area, which was profitable for the De Braoses. The town also became a Parliamentary Borough, with the right to elect two members of Parliament – first recorded in 1295. Originally it was only the owner-occupiers of fifty-two burgage plots, laid out around the Carfax and surrounding streets, who had the right to vote, but later burgage splitting and other malpractices crept in, and made Horsham a notorious 'rotten' borough in the eighteenth century. Horsham also gained status as it was a town where the judges came for the Assizes and Quarter Sessions from 1306 until 1830.

By 1600, Horsham was a flourishing market town well placed to service the Wealden iron industry, which produced guns for warfare and ploughshares for agriculture. After the decline of this industry, Horsham found a new role at the end of the eighteenth century as a staging post for the coaching trade, and a centre for traditional rural industries, such as tanning, brewing and brick-making. It was described as a most attractive town by visitors in the early nineteenth century. But the town suffered a considerable decline after the end of the Napoleonic Wars in 1815, and little was done to remedy this for the next fifty years. Horsham only faced up to long-standing problems of public health and local government after 1865. By the 1890s there were many improvements and a marked increase in civic spirit. Horsham was once again said to be 'a thriving and beautiful town'.

After the First World War, with a decline in the older rural industries, greatly improved road and rail services allowed people to live in Horsham and work elsewhere. Despite attempts to attract new light industries, and a considerable expansion in the 1950s, it seemed quite likely in the early 1960s that Horsham might become a mere suburb of the nearby new town of Crawley. Faced with this prospect, Horsham people accepted the need for dynamic measures to ensure the independent future of the town. Martin Pearson, the Chief Executive of Horsham District Council, said recently, 'Horsham is at a pivotal point in its history ... the challenge at the beginning of the century will be to complete the transformation begun in the 1970s from a small market town to that of a more substantial town, whilst maintaining the character of the town that has evolved during the centuries'.

Despite drastic and sometimes controversial changes, Horsham is still in essence the bustling market town it has been for more than seven centuries. Now the shops of Swan Walk and Pirie's Place have replaced the cattle, poultry and corn markets as the main hub of trade, while modern industries such as insurance, pharmaceuticals and electronics have brought new prosperity to the town. A dual carriageway has been built around the old town centre, which is now largely pedestrianized and free of the traffic which used to choke it. St Mark's Church has been demolished to make way for the new Royal & Sun Alliance headquarters, but its soaring spire has been retained. The redevelopment schemes have won several prestigious awards from the Civic Society and other bodies, including one for the imaginative way in which the old has been combined with the new. Inevitably the greatly increased size of the town and the influx of many new residents means that Horsham is no longer quite the tightly-knit community that it was in 1951, but in 1990 Horsham was called the 'top boom town of Britain', and in 2001 it is a very pleasant place in which to live.

Chapter 1

Horsham – A Town at a Crossroads

It is thought that the Saxon settlement of Horsham was built around this crossroads, in the tenth century or earlier. Denne Road, which goes past the Horse and Groom to the left, was the first north-south route through the town – it was probably a prehistoric track crossing the River Arun and going over Denne Hill. Here it meets East Street, which is part of the main east-west road through the town, coming from the coast and going on to Guildford and Oxford. This junction was called Stanestreet Cross in 1430, but there are indications of earlier buildings nearby and records of their inhabitants. Richard atte Stanstrete represented Horsham in Parliament from 1313 to 1322, and was listed as one of the town's wealthiest taxpayers at that time. The newsagent's shop on the left is part of an imposing medieval timber-framed house, which was called Bishop's in the sixteenth century. It had a central hall some 20ft long, which now houses a pizza restaurant, and was one of the original burgage houses.

The Tan bridge, so called because of a tannery which is known to have existed near here as early as 1424, is clearly seen in the foreground of the 1951 picture. This is the main bridge over the River Arun, on the road to Worthing, a seaside resort which developed rapidly after the opening of a new turnpike road over the South Downs from Findon in 1804. The main road from London passed through Horsham, and there were fourteen toll gates between Horsham and Worthing. One was at Tan Bridge, but the nearby toll gate, at the foot of Pict's Hill, was where travellers entering or leaving the town had to pay their dues. This gate was the scene of several tragic accidents, when horses drawing carts or carriages bolted down the hill, which was much steeper then than now. Before the gate was abolished in 1885, it was kept for many years by Mrs Jenny Hill, a feisty lady who would not let the cattle-drovers evade the tolls.

The 1951 view of the junction between the Carfax, Middle Street and East Street, with Market Square to the left, shows substantial differences from the modern photograph of the same crossroads. The medieval timber-framed building which can be seen in the centre of the 1951 photograph was then a well-known ironmongers shop called Glaysher's. When this site was redeveloped in the 1960s, the old building was carefully dismantled and re-erected at the Weald and Downland Museum, at Singleton. It is thought that it was originally used for smoking meat, because of the amount of soot found on the roofbeams – meat used to be preserved in this way in the days before refrigeration. Middle Street was known as Butchers' Row in the early nineteenth century because of the number of butchers' shops there, conveniently placed for the Carfax cattle market. The delivery boy's bicycle which peeps out from behind the corner of the King's Head Hotel on the right was still a common sight in Horsham in 1951.

There are not so many differences between the 1951 and modern views of the south side of the Carfax. Originally called *Scarfolkes*, a name apparently derived from 'scarce folk', the Carfax was a large open space, shaped like a funnel, used for holding markets and fairs from about 1300. It probably stretched right down to the Causeway in its earliest days. To begin with, temporary market stalls were put up there, but later permanent structures began to appear. Now there is a large island of buildings in the centre of the Carfax, which can be seen on the left, and blocks of buildings north and south of Middle Street, to the right. The Crown Hotel, built in 1805, can be seen in the right foreground of the 1951 photograph, while the King's Head Hotel, which was first mentioned as an inn in 1665, is at the centre of both in the background. Access to its yard for stagecoaches was improved in 1794 when a nearby cottage was pulled down.

The north side of the Carfax has now been pedestrianized and forms a pleasant area in which to sit out in summer. In the 1951 photograph, the pedimented building on the left was then the main office of King and Barnes, the Horsham brewers. The old Fountain Brewery, which dated back to the eighteenth century, formerly stood behind it. The building with rounded gables was the post office, while Grandford House beyond it was the family home of Henry Michell, a leading Horsham businessman, from 1841. Previously it was known as the Richmond Inn, and housed the Horsham Literary Institute. These buildings have now all been replaced with modern blocks, though Richmond Terrace, which took its name from the inn, has survived. In the eighteenth century, the Old Gaol, which was centred on the site of Grandford House, was condemned by John Howard, the prison reformer, who visited Horsham in 1774 and helped to prevent a prison breakout. In a damning report to Parliament he described the old Gaol as 'filthy and unsafe'.

This part of North Street, shown in the 1951 photograph, used to be mainly residential, containing large houses belonging to doctors and lawyers. Now it no longer exists – it has been replaced by a pedestrian walkway, Chart Way, which bridges Albion Way. The decision to build this new dual carriageway, which cuts through North Street and encircles the town centre, was one of the most controversial features of the redevelopment of the town centre in the 1980s. But it was as an essential part of the plan, to relieve the pressure of traffic going through the Carfax and the historic heart of the town. In the modern photograph, St Mark's Court, the headquarters of Royal & Sun Alliance, can be seen on the right. In 1964, the Sun Alliance and London Insurance Company, as it was then called, came to Horsham. The company originally operated from a large and intrusive skyscraper in North Street, but in the 1980s, Sun Alliance built a new 'campus' on both sides of Albion Way.

The North Street junction with Park Street, on the left, was long known as 'Chart's Corner', and this is how Chart Way got its name. Amos Chart the corn merchant had a shop in Park Street in the 1890s, which later became the Model Shop. On the right is the Hurst Arms, which has now taken the name of an earlier pub, the Black Jug (or Jack). In the eighteenth century the Black Jack was probably in the older building next door, which was also used as a boarding school by Richard Thornton. The diarist John Baker saw 'a man drunk and people about him near the Black Jack' on 27 April 1773. He discovered that the man was Farmer Miller, who said that the schoolmaster had got into bed with his daughter, aged sixteen, during the previous night. She was clearly a resourceful girl, as she had climbed out of the window and made her way home to her father's house in the country in the dark! Richard Thornton later ran a boy's school in the Old Gaol in the Carfax.

The present Horsham railway station was built in 1938, when the Southern Railway was electrified. This was the third station to be built in North Street since the railway came to Horsham in 1848. Originally Horsham was the terminus of a branch line from Three Bridges, but in 1857 this line was extended to Pulborough, and later to Portsmouth. There was a previous station on this site, built in 1859, but the first station was on the other side of North Street. Horsham was an important railway junction in 1892, when it was already said to be 'an especially convenient centre for tourists'. The railway was responsible for changing the whole pattern of trade in mid-Sussex; goods could be brought in from all over the country, and this seriously affected local industries. It was feared that Horsham might become a dormitory town between the Wars, as people could quite easily live here and work in London. Many people still commute, but now there are greatly increased employment opportunities in Horsham.

These views of the railway station from the road bridge show that the basic layout remains much the same today as it was in 1951. Horsham has a choice of two routes to London, via Dorking or Three Bridges. In 1860, a branch line was built from Horsham to Guildford, but this was closed in 1965, as part of the Beeching plan for rationalising the railway system. In 1951, Horsham was still a major rail junction with connections to Brighton via Shoreham and to Petworth via Pulborough, as well as those to Bognor Regis, Chichester and Portsmouth which still operate. The lines to Petworth and Shoreham fell victim to the cuts brought about by the huge development of road traffic in the latter half of the twentieth century. However, the railway is still important to Horsham, and existing stations at Christ's Hospital, Ifield and Faygate may well be a crucial factor in deciding where future large-scale housing development in the area will be situated.

These views from the end of East Street look towards the Iron Bridge where the railway crosses the road. In the past this was called Upper East Street. Queen Street only runs from the bridge to the corner of New Street. The railway was built right though the site of the last Horsham Gaol, which was demolished in 1845 after it had been sold to Henry Michell, a local brewer. He re-used the millions of bricks he recovered for several other buildings and the Three Bridges railway embankment. When the line going south to Pulborough was built in 1857, the road was lowered so that traffic could pass under the bridge, but modern double-decker buses and tall lorries now have to take another route. Few of the Victorian houses, which were standing on the right-hand side of the photograph in 1951, remain today. Now the link road, Park Way, has been built through to Albion Way, as shown by the modern road signs on the left.

In these views of New Street looking north, at the junction with Victoria Street and Bedford Road, the modern photograph shows that there has been some rebuilding of the southern part of New Street, which runs from Station Road down to Queen Street. This part of the town began to be developed shortly after the enclosure of Horsham Common in 1812. New Street was built on what was previously called Pest House Lane. As early as 1774, John Baker, the diarist, wrote of a house on the common, run by Doctor Linfield, which was used for the isolation of several of his servants who had been inoculated against smallpox – this is maybe what gave the lane its name. Tanneries, brickfields and other commercial enterprises existed in this area, north of Brighton Road, even before the 1812 enclosure. William Cobbett complained in 1823 that Horsham Common was 'cut up, disfigured, spoiled, and the labourers driven from its skirts', but the town needed space to develop these industries.

The crossroads at the far end of West Street, where Springfield Road met Worthing Road, with the Bishopric to the west, was a major road junction in 1951. It was known as Black Horse Corner, after the hotel and former coaching inn which stood at the end of West Street, but has an even longer history. In 1411 it was called Lynd Cross and it is known that there was a dovecote in the garden of a house nearby. The name has now been revived and given to the pub on the right in the later picture. In the eighteenth century, John Shelley planned to build a mansion where McDonald's is now, but only built some stables which later became the West Street Brewery, leased by Henry Michell. The arch which can be seen in the 1951 picture, behind the car showroom, was part of the brewery. In the 1990s, this area was pedestrianized and adorned with the Shelley Fountain, which commemorates the poet Percy Bysshe Shelley, great-nephew of John.

This junction at the foot of the bridge over the railway line, north of the station, was known as Agate's Corner in 1951. Agate's timberyard to the right of the photograph has now been replaced by a large office development, called Horsham Gates. These buildings were completed just before the 1991 recession, but it was not until they were all occupied in 1995 that Horsham was said to have recovered fully from this economic setback. When Station Road, on the left, was originally built in the 1840s, it went straight into North Street opposite the original station. It was diverted northwards when the second station was built on the east side of North Street in 1859, following the opening of the line to the south. Station Road originally passed between two small farms, called Hamper's Farm and Fillery's Farm, shown on the 1840 Tithe map. One of the old farmhouse buildings, timber-framed with a Horsham stone roof, can still be seen today behind the present station.

This junction of three roads – North Parade in the foreground, London Road to the left and Springfield Road to the right – was known as Potter's Corner in 1951. Mrs Potter had a sweet shop on the corner, and George Potter the builder had his premises on the other side of London Road. Further down London Road can be seen Brunswick Place and Sussex Terrace, an elegant row of Georgian townhouses, built around 1835. In 1841, the tenants included a future vicar of Horsham, two doctors and an aspiring businessman. This used to be the main road from London into Horsham, and as such it now contains a very varied selection of buildings, from different periods and styles. It has suffered from being cut off from the Carfax by Albion Way, and has not benefited from the carefully planned redevelopment of the town centre. The commercial office block and video superstore which has now been built on this corner is considered by many to be unsightly and out of scale.

These photographs are of Roffey Corner, an important junction on the east side of Horsham. The original Roffey was a hamlet nearly two miles to the north-east of this corner, lying along the main road to Crawley pictured in the 1951 photograph. It is thought that the name Roffey derived from *rogh hay*, which means deer park, and there is evidence that such a park existed here in the fourteenth century. Traces have also been found of a large medieval house and a bloomery, or iron-working site, beyond Roffey Park. By 1840, Star Row, which contained an inn and a tollgate, with a smock mill nearby, had been built to the west of Roffey Corner, in Crawley Road. This area became part of Roffey, and is now at the heart of the civil parish of North Horsham. To the right is the road to Pease Pottage, through St Leonard's Forest, where travellers were supposedly given pease pottage (thick pea soup) at the gatehouse.

This level crossing in Parsonage Road, in an apparently quiet and leafy lane, is actually at the centre of Horsham's industrial estates. In 1951, the crossing was controlled by the keeper who lived in the house shown in the earlier photograph, and the gates were closed at night. Now the crossing is worked automatically. Behind the trees are the UK headquarters of Novartis, one of the world's largest pharmaceutical groups. The Swiss firm, CIBA, established its British headquarters and laboratories in Horsham in 1938, and built a research unit there in the 1960s. It amalgamated with Geigy, another Swiss firm, before becoming part of Novartis in the 1990s. CIBA came to Horsham following a determined attempt by the then Horsham Urban District Council to diversify the town's economy between the two World Wars. Several light engineering firms were set up in the 1930s in Foundry Lane, off Parsonage Road. Now the industrial estates have expanded into Redkiln Way and there are new businesses based on electronics and computer technology.

Chapter 2

Markets and Market Places

The 1951 photograph shows the Carfax, the original market place of the town. By 1800 there was a regular Saturday corn market, said to have been originally granted by King John, and a cattle market, granted by Queen Anne in 1705, which was held on the last Tuesday of every month. There were also four fairs held here during the year: sheep were sold at the April and July fairs; cattle in the week before Whitsun; and horses in November. The July fair was the most important, and provided the townsfolk with a rare opportunity for fun and entertainment, with its stalls and sideshows. In his first known letter, written at the age of ten, Percy Bysshe Shelley asked his cousin Tom Medwin to 'bring me a fairing, which is some gingerbread, sweetmeat, hunting-nuts and a pocket-book'. There is now a local produce and farmers' market in the Carfax on Saturdays, and occasional funfairs, but the shopping centres of Swan Walk and Pirie's Place have become the chief focus of trade.

The 1951 view of the west side of Market Square shows Attwater's Sports House, where the *West Sussex County Times* now has its office, on the right. A late seventeenth-century inn, called the Half Moon, used to stand on this site, next to the Bear. Market Square was the place where the farmers' wives and traders would come to sell their butter, eggs, and fattened poultry, on market and fair days. They would set up their stalls in the arcade of the Market Hall, a square building raised on arches in the centre of the Square, which has now been replaced by the rather larger Town Hall, seen on the left. In 1759, Sarah Hurst, the daughter of a tailor, was working in her father's shop, on the other side of Market Square. She complained of the endless noise and bustle of fair days, but enjoyed the company of her friend and confidante, Sally Sheppard, who lived in the old Half Moon, while she waited for the man she loved, Capt. Henry Smith, to return from the Seven Years' War. They married secretly in Slinfold in 1762, and Capt. Smith became Colonel Commandant of the Marine Corps at Portsmouth in 1772. Widowed in 1794, Sarah returned to Horsham and spent the last years of her life at Causeway House, now the home of Horsham Museum, which can be seen in the background of both photographs.

The King's Head Hotel, on the corner of the Carfax and East Street, and the Anchor Hotel on the east side of Market Square – the tall building with a pediment – are little changed in appearance since 1951. The King's Head has been Horsham's best-known hostelry since the seventeenth century, while the Anchor Hotel, built in 1885 to replace the Anchor Inn, is now a wine bar, though it housed the National Provincial Bank in 1951. Market Square was where Parliamentary elections took place, and both inns played their part. In 1790, the Tory supporters of Lady Irwin used the King's Head as their headquarters, while the Duke of Norfolk and his Whigs patronized the Anchor. Both sides sought support by providing lavish venison feasts, and plying those entitled to vote with drink. It was said, 'Who would not be a burgess of Horsham, where cobblers are treated like Kings?' The election was shamelessly rigged by the Duke's agents, but Lady Irwin's candidates eventually won on petition.

The Bank Buildings in the Carfax, built in 1897, were designed by a noted London architect, Frederick Wheeler FRIBA, who had an office here in Horsham. He designed other bank buildings in Sussex as well as Sussex House in Tooting. The Horsham Club, a prestigious lunch club, is housed in this building. The Carfax has long been the home of professional firms, such as lawyers' offices and banks, as well as a market place. The later photograph shows how the bandstand has been moved slightly to the right from its position in 1951. The war memorial, which lay on the east side of the Carfax in 1951, has also been relocated, and placed in the new pedestrianized area. The 1980s redevelopment has ensured that the Carfax remains at the heart of the town, and its principal public meeting place. Horsham's well-known Cheese Shop and a high-class butcher and greengrocer are among the few independent local stores remaining here, while branches of nationwide estate agents and building societies have proliferated.

In this 1951 view looking down on the Carfax, towards the north-west corner, the small buildings at the top have now all disappeared with the building of Swan Walk, the town's main shopping mall. The entrance to Swan Walk can just be seen in the modern photograph. In 1951, the Horsham Market building behind the bus housed the Women's Institute weekly market, which started up in 1932 and was the first of its kind in the country. On the top right, the large building on the corner of London Road (now Medwin Walk) was a large coaching inn, called the Lamb. It is now the offices of King and Chasemore, an estate and land agency founded here over 100 years ago. Horsham was an important staging post for the coaches which clattered through the town daily on their way to or from London, Brighton, Worthing, Guildford and Oxford in the early nineteenth century. Now the pedestrianisation of this side of the Carfax has freed it from noise and traffic.

In the 1951 view of the north side of West Street, local businesses, like that of A. Hull and Son, fruiterer and florist, still predominated. Now most of the shops can be seen in any other high street. West Street was one of the town's earliest market places; in 1449 King Henry VI granted a Charter for the holding of a market every Monday in '*le Weststrete*' which became the poultry market. It has been the principal shopping street of the town for the last 200 years. In the modern picture, the West Street entrance to Swan Walk can just be seen beyond the white building. In 1951, the Swan Hotel stood here. Sir Bysshe Shelley was said to have frequented the Swan to hear the local gossip when he was living in Horsham around 1810. In 1836, the *Star* coach driven by Bob Whittle, Horsham's smartest coachman, left the Swan Inn for London every morning at 7 a.m. (except Sunday), arriving back at 8 p.m.

In 1862, West Street became the home of the corn market, moved from Saturdays to Wednesdays, to bring it in line with the new cattle market in the Bishopric. An impressive Italianate Corn Exchange, designed by the Horsham architect Edward Burstow, was built in 1866, next door to the Black Horse Hotel. It contained corn stores and a market room, as well as an assembly room. The Corn Exchange closed in 1913, and was absorbed into the hotel. Both were demolished in 1964, when shops and offices were built on the site. The whole area was pedestrianized during the second stage of the redevelopment of the town centre, begun in 1995. It is now dominated by the Shelley Fountain, designed by Angela Conner, which was called *Rising Universe*, when it was unveiled in November 1996, with reference to the opening lines of Shelley's poem *Mont Blanc*. It has since been renamed *Cosmic Cycle*, after some controversy about the design. In the foreground, there is a landscaped water garden.

In 1951, the Central Market lay to the east of the Carfax, behind what is now the Waitrose supermarket. In the background can be seen Pirie's Place, a row of fifteen Victorian cottages, built around 1860 at a cost of about £130 each, by William Pirie, the headmaster of Collyer's School. The cottages, decorated with the Scottish thistle as he was a Scotsman, were built as a commercial speculation, probably to provide Mr Pirie with some extra income for his retirement. However, he died in harness in 1868 after a lifetime devoted to teaching the poorer children of Horsham. It is known that he enjoyed giving Bonfire Night parties, to which he invited all his friends, but his wife alienated even her own family. William Pirie is now appropriately commemorated with a bronze sculpture, by Lorne McKean, which shows him in the donkey cart he habitually drove around Horsham, in the new Pirie's Place shopping centre. The sculpture is very popular, especially with young children, who climb happily all over it.

The top photograph shows Pirie's Place as it was in 1951 – a row of houses, with pedestrian access, between the Carfax and Park Street. The new Pirie's Place built in 1990, includes the Waitrose supermarket, on the left in the modern photograph, which retains an existing frontage onto the Carfax. Pirie's Place, with its sunny courtyard, is now a pleasant place in which to shop or have a snack. Until recently, it hosted a small craft market on Thursdays and Saturdays, but this has now been moved. A new walkway was opened in December 2000, to link Pirie's Place with East Street. It was named Stan's Way to commemorate Stan Parsons, who kept a newsagent's shop in the Carfax for forty-three years from 1929. He raised money to buy a Spitfire during the Second World War, which was always known as Stan's Spitfire. He also served as an independent town councillor and was tirelessly active in so many aspects of Horsham life that he was eventually nicknamed 'Mr Horsham'.

In 1852 a new cattle market, held on alternate Wednesdays, was established here in the Bishopric, west of the junction with Springfield Road. The road was wide enough for cattle pens to be erected on either side. By 1900, the market was held every Wednesday, and cheap trains were run to Horsham on market day. The market flourished until increasing motor traffic made it impossible for it to be held here. The 1951 photograph shows how many old cottages still survived in the Bishopric. Life there in the 1930s was unforgettably described by Henry Burstow, the well-known shoemaker, singer and bell-ringer, in his *Reminiscences of Horsham*. The tall trees on the right housed the rooks who were said to have given the Bishopric its nickname of 'the Rookery', though Burstow said that this name might also have come from the noisy squabbles of its inhabitants. The modern photograph shows the new buildings east of the King's Arms which have replaced the old cottages where Burstow was born in 1826.

In the 1951 view from the railway bridge, a few animal pens can be seen in the foreground. At this time the cattle market, combined with the poultry market, was held in the old goods yard near the station, in Nightingale Road, but it was in its dying days. In the 1960s, centralised wholesale marketing in Croydon replaced all the local North Sussex markets. Now Nightingale Road, named after the family who owned the local Lambsbottom Farm and brickworks in the nineteenth century, is a place for motor repair shops and warehouses. So, in the strict sense of the word, Horsham is no longer a 'market' town, but it remains a place of trade and commerce, with its new retail shopping centres taking the place of the old markets and fairs. People still come in from the surrounding area to buy what they need, as they have done for seven centuries or more. In that sense, Horsham has retained its essential character through all the changes that have taken place.

This part of Springfield Road, which used to join London Road at North Parade, was a rather run-down commercial area in 1951. The former Congregational Chapel can be seen in the middle distance. It is now part of a pedestrianized area between the Shelley Fountain and Albion Way. Surprisingly, it is also Horsham's latest marketplace. When the traders who used to have their stalls in Pirie's Place were given notice to quit in October 2000, the council found a new home for them here and on the other side of the Shelley Fountain. The final stage of the town centre redevelopment, due to be completed in 2003, will be the creation of a new 'Millennium Square' to the south of this area, where there will be a large department store, shops and housing, as well as the existing Library. This should complete the transformation of Horsham from an old-fashioned country market town, which it was in 1951, to a modern town centre with a wide range of facilities.

Chapter 3

Streets and Buildings

This view of the Causeway has changed very little since 1951, and it is one of the most attractive and well-preserved streets in Sussex. Percy Bysshe Shelley would have known a very similar street scene two centuries ago, when he was growing up here. Most of the houses are originally medieval timber-framed buildings, but some were refronted in the eighteenth century. Those on the right are roofed with hard-wearing Horsham stone, which gives a local character to the houses here. William Cobbett said when he visited Horsham in 1823 that it was, 'a very nice, solid country town. Very clean, as all the towns in Sussex are. The people very clean. The Sussex women are very nice in their dress and in their houses. The men and boys wear smock-frocks more than they do in some counties'. It is perhaps fortunate that Horsham was not more prosperous during the Victorian period, as many more of its old buildings might well have been destroyed had there been funds available for modernisation then.

St Mary's church, built around 1247 as the parish church and expanded in later centuries, is the oldest building in Horsham. In the 1951 view from the Causeway a slight difference in camera angle has dramatically increased the apparent height of the spire. This familiar crooked landmark is twice recorded as having been struck by lightning which set its wooden shingles on fire – in 1615 a girl called Elizabeth Stroode was also said to have been killed 'as she stood by the belfry door'. A significant event took place in the church on 18 November 1830, during the 'Captain Swing' uprising throughout the south-east of England, when local agricultural labourers, who were suffering great hardship, formed a mob of more than 700 men and converged upon the building. Supported by many townspeople, they forced the vicar and Robert Hurst, the lay rector, to agree to their demands for a living wage and lower tithes. But dragoons were called in and the agitation was effectively suppressed. The house on the right of both photographs, called The Chantry, is thought to have originally been the barn of the house belonging to the chaplain who served Butler's Chantry in St Mary's church, before all chantries were closed down in 1550. The Chantry was the home, in 1939, of Sir Hartley Shawcross, later the chief British prosecutor of Nazi war criminals at the Nuremburg trials, and President of the Board of Trade.

The east end of St Mary's church is here seen from Normandy, a road which contains an ancient well, said to be remarkably pure and unfailing, although only 4ft deep. The church was restored in 1864 and 1865 at a cost of £8,000 by S.S. Teulon, who performed an extraordinary engineering feat in jacking-up the walls to correct a pronounced lean, caused by the building of a gallery on the south side. Now Horsham's only Grade I listed building, St Mary's church is in the midst of another major programme of restoration and conservation, estimated to cost well over £1 million. There was a bell foundry in Normandy between 1592 and 1623, owned by Richard Eldridge, who cast bells for Horsham and elsewhere in Sussex. The art of bell-ringing has long been practised here, and there was a notable team of bell-ringers in Horsham from 1766 to 1798, who established several records for

ringing Grandsire or Union Triples. Henry Burstow was also a noted bell-ringer, and he and his fellow shoemakers rang a 'shoemakers' peal' all day long on his wedding day in 1855. The almshouses, which have been rebuilt since 1951, can be seen on the left of both photographs. Previously there was a parish workhouse on this site, built in 1725. John Baker saw the workhouse children 'playing, sprawling and tumbling about like little puppies' when he walked through the churchyard on 20 May 1773.

In these views from South Street down the Causeway, the house on the left, Causeway Lodge, is part of an original burgage site known as Hadmans, which includes the timber-framed building in the centre. This gives access through an archway to Morth Gardens, originally the boundary between the borough and land belonging to the Church. Dorothea Hurst, who published the first comprehensive history of Horsham anonymously in 1868, lived at Causeway Lodge. Morth Gardens was named after John Morth the carpenter, who built three cottages there for his daughters. Behind the wall on the right is the Manor House, built by Nathaniel Tredcroft in 1704 after he had married an heiress. His descendants were regarded as 'squires' of Horsham until young Edward Tredcroft borrowed beyond his means from the lawyer Henry Padwick, who foreclosed on him, taking possession of the Manor House in the 1850s. Since then, the building has housed Manor House School (there in 1951) and the national headquarters of the RSPCA, which moved to Southwater in 2001.

It would seem that the Causeway has long been tree-lined, from the evidence of a map from 1770 which clearly depicts two rows of trees. It was said in 1814 that Horsham, although 'not large' had a 'rural appearance, trees being planted each side of the streets ... the visitor on his first entry into the place is struck with its appearance'. In 1940, new trees were planted; which were still small in 1951 but are now so tall that they have been lopped. The two buildings on the right were both built in the fifteenth century in the Wealden style – the one that has been refronted in brick belonged for a time to Sir Timothy Shelley and was occupied by his former butler. It was leased to William Pirie, the headmaster of Collyer's, while the school was being rebuilt in 1840. Thomas Picke, a barber-surgeon carrying on the trade of his father and grandfather, lived in the weather-boarded house on the right until his death in 1681.

The Town Hall is one of Horsham's most unusual buildings, and was built on the site of the old arcaded Market House. The Market House used to be boarded up for use as a courtroom when the Assizes were held in Horsham in the eighteenth century, but the judges found it too cold and draughty. In 1812, the 11th Duke of Norfolk had the building converted into a town hall at a cost of £8,000, with a courtroom on each floor and rooms for the judges and jury. The 15th Duke sold the freehold to the town for £25 in 1888, and the old building was demolished and rebuilt, except for the north wall which bore the Royal arms, together with those of the Dukes of Norfolk and Horsham. In 1951, the Town Hall was still being used as a council chamber and magistrates' court. John George Haigh, who committed the 'acid bath murders' in Crawley, appeared before the magistrates here in 1949, before standing trial. At that time, the Town Hall was also used to count the votes and announce the results of elections, which had traditionally been held here in the days of the Borough. Now a new court house has been built in Hurst Road and the election count takes place at Collyer's Sixth Form College. The Town Hall now houses the registry office. Regular book and antique fairs, and art and craft shows, are held there.

In the 1951 view of West Street looking east, the large spectacles which hung outside Jury Cramp's shop can be seen on the right – they proclaimed him to be an optician as well as a jeweller, and are now hanging in the trades gallery in Horsham Museum. Jury Cramp was trained as a watchmaker and goldsmith in Clerkenwell, and named his shop Clerkenwell House when he rebuilt it in 1878. A small man, only 5ft tall, he was very active in the Temperance movement and many other local organisations. Wakefield's Café on the right was a popular place to meet in 1951, and the Wakefield family ran a number of businesses, of which a jeweller's shop and a high-class clothes shop still bear their name in West Street. Henry Burstow listed all the West Street shops and their owners in 1830, when they kept very long hours and were only illuminated with tallow dips or rushlights. The pedestrianisation of West Street has freed it from noise and car fumes.

Not a great deal appears to have changed since 1951 in these views of the oldest part of East Street, but much has been done lately to restore the medieval timber-framed buildings on the north side of the road. The East Street frontage to Stan's Way, a new alleyway through to Pirie's Place, has been carefully reconstructed by Horsham District Council, based on a detailed archaeological study. East Street has a long history, and has played an important part in the development of the town. Dr Annabelle Hughes has found evidence that the monks of the Abbey of Fécamp owned commercial premises in East Street which were let out to tradesmen as early as the fourteenth century. It is known that there was a monk called Vigor who served as bailiff to the Abbot of Fécamp in 1341, and there was a property on the south side of East Street called Vigor's Mead. East Street retains two local businesses which were there in 1951: Trelfer's the jewellers and Scott and Sargeant.

In the 1951 view of Middle Street looking east, the Punchbowl Café, on the site of an old inn of the same name, is on the left, and behind it the premises of James Lea the tailor, who had been in business there since the 1880s. The Punchbowl Café had very low ceilings and customers were warned as they entered to 'Mind your head'! On the right was the department store, Tanner and Chart, but their claim to have been established in 1784 does not appear to be borne out by the early trade directories. This very narrow street is important as it links West Street and East Street, but it was one of the first one-way streets in Horsham, as it was impossible for two carts to pass each other there. During the Second World War, tanks trying to drive down the street would get their tracks wedged between the pavements. Now pedestrianized, it remains as a shopping street with an interesting variety of stores.

This is all that now remains of South Street, which used to include the Causeway and Market Square, as noted in the land tax records of the old borough. Evershed and Cripps, the well-known local high-class grocers, were still in business in 1951, as seen on the left. This was one of the first shops in Horsham to put up Christmas decorations, with an illuminated Father Christmas on the roof. The old crane, used to hoist goods up to the storeroom, can still be seen on the outside of the building. The two small houses in the centre of the photograph were built in the 1770s by Thomas Griffiths, with bricks supposedly rejected for the building of Horsham Gaol. The house at the end was the Red Lion Bookshop in 1951 – formerly an inn. It is now the Horsham Christian Centre, a coffee shop and bookshop run by volunteers from several local churches. The Victorian Gothic building on the right originally housed the Capital and Counties Bank, and is now Lloyds TSB.

The spire of the former St Mark's church, which was built in 1870, remains at the heart of the new Royal & Sun Alliance 'campus' in Chart Way. The spire, a much loved landmark, was saved by a vigorous protest campaign but the disused church, built in 1840, was pulled down in 1989 as part of the redevelopment scheme. A new St Mark's church was built in North Heath Lane, where it is now serving the greatly enlarged community of North Horsham. The building in the centre of the 1951 photograph now fronts the Waitrose supermarket. On the left is a building which is much older than it looks. It is known to have been called the Gaoler's House in the early part of the seventeenth century. It was part of Horsham's first Gaol; the actual prison was just behind it in North Street, while the second, known later as the Old Gaol, was on the north side of the Carfax from 1640 to 1775.

This is the view of North Street, looking south-west towards the town centre, which greets the visitor to Horsham coming out of the station, with St Mark's spire as a distant landmark. The little group of old cottages clearly seen in the 1951 photograph have nearly all survived and been incorporated into a new and sympathetically-designed housing development on the edge of Horsham Park, which provides a pleasant green space in the heart of the town. Park House, the former home of the Hurst family and now the headquarters of Horsham District Council, is hidden behind the trees in the centre. North Street was sometimes called Comewell Street in the seventeenth century, taking its name from a public well situated there. In the modern photograph, part of the new Royal & Sun Alliance development can be seen in the distance, where North Street becomes Chart Way. Since coming to Horsham in 1964, the company has contributed enormously to the town's prosperity, and is now its major commercial employer.

The 1951 view of London Road from the Carfax shows the forecourt of the Capitol theatre on the left and, in the centre, the medieval burgage house called Bornes, which was pulled down in the 1960s when Swan Walk was first built. The house next to Bornes was occupied by Cotchings the solicitors, who were given some papers of Thomas Charles Medwin and his son Pilfold, whose office was just across the road. The two Medwins served as lawyers in Horsham from 1776 to 1880, and both took a very active part in the town's affairs. William Albery had earlier acquired the bulk of the Medwin papers and bequeathed them to the town in 1950. They now form the basis of the Museum's archive collections. This part of London Road, cut off from the rest by Albion Way, has been renamed Medwin Walk. Swan Walk shopping mall looms on the left of the modern picture, while the new buildings on the right adjoin King and Chasemore, which faces on to the Carfax.

The 1951 photograph of Springfield Road shows the Catholic church on the left and the forecourt of the former Congregational church on the right. In the centre of the photograph can be seen the Michell Arms, named after Henry Michell the brewer, who was one of Horsham's leading businessmen in the nineteenth century. It now lies on the far side of Albion Way and has been renamed the Malt Shovel. Springfield Road used to be called Chapel Lane because it housed Pastor Harm's Chapel, which was built in 1814 on a piece of land taken from Swan Meadow. Later this chapel was rebuilt as the Congregational church, but it had to be pulled down when Albion Way was built in the 1980s. Now the United Reform church has been built within the development on the right. A new presbytery now adjoins the Catholic church, but St John's Catholic School, which lay to the right of the church in 1951, has been rebuilt off Blackbridge Lane.

This part of the Worthing Road has played an important part in the history of the town as it contains two of Horsham's earliest nonconformist places of worship. The General Baptist Chapel (now the Unitarian church), which was built in 1721, lies behind the row of cottages which bear an advertisement for the Punchbowl Café in the 1951 photograph. The Friends' Meeting House, successor to one built in 1693, is just to the left in both photographs. Many Quakers suffered imprisonment in Horsham Gaol from 1655 to 1685, but their leader Ambrose Rigge, who was held for more than ten years, emerged even stronger in his faith. The Baptist church was founded by several local families, notably the Caffyns, Dendys and Eversheds, who were among the earliest elders and ministers. By 1892 it had become divided from the General Baptist Assembly and was known as the Free Christian Church. It was thanks to the then minister, the Revd J.J. Marten, that Horsham Museum Society was founded in 1893.

The Queen Street post office used to be within Stanley's bread shop on the corner of New Street in 1951, but its sign can now be seen on the right side of the road where there was a public house called The Plume of Feathers. At New Street, Queen Street becomes Brighton Road, which runs from here to the south-eastern outskirts of the town. The Brighton Road Baptist church in the centre of both photographs was founded in 1894, but the present building was completed in 1923. The small house in front of the church is similar to the cottages in Morth's Gardens and may have been built by John Morth, who died in 1827. Brighton Road was used by stagecoaches on their way from London to Brighton via Henfield, where another road led to Shoreham, one of the main ports in Sussex. Now Horsham lies between two major dual carriageways linking London with the coast, so Brighton Road is no longer as important a thoroughfare as it once was.

Chapter 4

Industries Old and New

This tranquil scene at the entrance to St Leonard's Forest, from Hamper's Lane, gives no hint of the activity which used to be carried out here. Horsham was the centre for the iron industry of the western Weald, with forges at Warnham, Shipley and in St Leonard's Forest. Much of the town's prosperity in the fifteenth and sixteenth centuries depended on it. Heavy waggons, drawn by oxen, would have trundled constantly up and down this road, bringing in iron ore and charcoal to the forges and foundries, and bringing out the iron which was cast into the guns which defeated the Spanish Armada, or made into nails, horseshoes and firebacks. Many of the gentry who ruled Horsham and the surrounding area in the seventeenth century made their fortunes in this industry. In the eighteenth century the roads through the forest were used by smugglers to run their goods from the coast – some of the legends concerned with the forest were probably invented at this time to keep people away!

A medieval farm house called Netherledys remains in Needles Close, but Needles Farm shown in 1951 now lies beneath a housing estate built by Horsham Urban District Council around 1960 – the building next to the youth centre was a cowshed in 1951. Some of the old field names have been retained – one of the roads in this area is called Jockey Mead, which appears on the 1840 Tithe map. Needles was the original name of the farm, though it was called Tan Bridge Farm in 1840. It formed part of the estate owned by Henry Ellis of Tanbridge House in the late eighteenth century. He died young, in 1785, and his widow married Robert Killick. Henry Burstow said that Mrs Killick was the last person to be buried in a night funeral in Horsham, in 1829. There was a preference for night funerals among some of the wealthier members of society, and they were spectacular occasions, with the burial performed in the light of flaring torches.

The 1951 photograph is of Bennett's Farm, which lay to the north of the Brighton Road, just west of what is now St Leonard's Road. Bennett's Farm originally stretched from the tanyard on the west to what is now Comptons Lane on the east, and in 1840 it was owned by Sir Henry Fletcher, the third baronet, who also owned the large Lintott estates in Southwater, inherited from his grandmother Catherine Lintott. The field on the corner of St Leonard's Road was being used as a small nursery garden by Frederick Allman. He later had a much larger nursery on the north side of East Street, which covered ten acres to the east of what is now Park Place, and was called Allman's Corner. Bennett's Farm has given its name to Bennett's Field recreation ground, and the buildings that can be seen in the modern photograph are the changing rooms. The name Higgins Way commemorates Brian Higgins, of Higgins and Edwards the builders, who founded the 5th Horsham Scout troop.

These buildings have been identified as Highlands Farm, which still existed in 1951 in the southern part of Comptons Lane, near its junction with St Leonard's Road. It was a very old farm – Sarah Hurst mentions walking with her mother and aunts to 'Papa's farm Highland' on 1 April 1759. It was rented by Richard Hurst, who probably let it to a sub-tenant as he was a working tailor. His son Robert, a successful lawyer, became Horsham's largest land owner when he bought up most of Horsham Common after its enclosure in 1812. Highlands Farm was owned by Guildford Hospital in 1840. It bordered Smithsbarn Farm in what was then called Smithsbarn Lane. The Queen Elizabeth II Silver Jubilee School, for children with severe learning difficulties, has now been built in place of Highlands Farm. It is set back from the road, behind the houses bordering Comptons Lane, which appear in the modern picture. The Forest Community School now covers what was Smithsbarn Farm.

Lambsbottom Farm in Hurst Road survived as a working farm into the 1930s, surprisingly close to the Horsham station. It was a small dairy farm kept by the Nightingale family, who also owned a brickyard nearby. Mrs. Nightingale ran the dairy business. The farmhouse shown in the modern photograph has survived and is now used as an office, while the farm buildings shown in the 1951 photograph have mainly disappeared or been rebuilt. This area was called Bowling Green in the nineteenth century, and there is still a lane with that name off Hurst Road. There was a bowling alley here where John Baker used to go to play with his friends, when living nearby at Park House. One of the first things he did when he came to Horsham in 1771 was to order a set of bowls, and he appears to have played to win. On one occasion he admitted that his partner, the Rev. Thomas White, had cheated their opponents in reckoning up the score!

This is the old Town Mill, which is probably the oldest mill in Horsham, on the River Arun below the church. The mill belonged to Rusper Nunnery for more than three centuries, since it is mentioned in the deed for the endowment of Horsham church in 1231, and in 1532 the Nunnery rent rolls mention a watermill here. By 1742, it belonged to Edward Tredcroft, who leased it to William and Resta Patching on the understanding that they would supply the town with piped water from the River Arun. Some wooden pipes, now in Horsham Museum, were laid in South Street, but by 1745 Resta had been declared bankrupt. In 1756, the lease was taken over by John Smart, timber merchant, millwright and landlord of the Dog and Bacon, and John Michell, plumber. John Smart bequeathed his interest in the mill and the waterworks to his son-in-law, Stringer Sheppard, the butcher, in 1771. Stringer and his son William were recorded as millers until 1844. The building is now used as offices.

Prewett's mill in Worthing Road was built by Henry Allberry, miller of the Town Mill, in 1861, and was later acquired by William Prewett, who bought the Town Mill in about 1890 and ran the two in conjunction. The Prewett family built up a business as millers and corn merchants, but they also ran a dairy in North Parade, and had started the Arun Engineering Company by 1905. Its most famous product was the Arun sawbench which was supplied to the Government during the Second World War. In 1951, the mill's output of stone-ground flour was 1,289 tons, most of which was delivered throughout Sussex, Surrey and London by the firm's fleet of two vans and six lorries. Prewett's bakery in West Street produced about 7,600 loaves a week and supplied Christ's Hospital School and London retailers. The firm was bought out by Allinsons in the early 1970s and the mill was closed in 1978. In 1983 the buildings were restored and became part of the Allied Domecq offices.

The sign of the Green Dragon, in the foreground of this 1951 photograph of the Bishopric, advertises 'Horsham Fine Ales' brewed at the nearby King and Barnes Brewery. King and Barnes was formed from the merger of two well-known local brewers in the early part of the twentieth century. There was a long tradition of brewing in Horsham, which at one time had fifty public houses, but in the year 2000, King and Barnes was bought out by a Dorset brewer and closed down. It was the last large brewery in the town and produced real ales, so its closure was viewed with general dismay. But the story of brewing in Horsham is not yet finished. In 2001, two companies have been launched to produce the much-loved Horsham beers elsewhere in the town. In the modern photograph, this part of the Bishopric is now bisected by Albion Way, and an attractive water garden has been created in the area in front of the Green Dragon.

The 1951 photograph shows a terrace of cottages in New Town, an area developed in the 1830s almost certainly to provide cheap rented accommodation for the workers at a large tanyard on the other side of the Brighton Road. This was a good site for tanning as it was built around ponds linked by a stream, which provided the water needed for steeping and washing the hides during the tanning process. It was, at that time, outside the main part of the town, which was necessary as tanning was a smelly business! A large cast-iron building, brought from Bermondsey where the Moons, who owned the tannery, had family connections, has been preserved and re-erected at the Amberley Chalk Pits Industrial Museum. Tanning was central to Horsham's traditional economy – the monthly cattle markets provided a regular supply of hides, and the tanyard supplied shoemakers, glovers and saddlers in Horsham with leather to pursue their various crafts. The modern photograph shows that the old cottages have all disappeared.

The 1951 photograph shows the brickyard in Queen Street, abandoned in 1939. It was one of many brickyards established in Horsham in the nineteenth century. Queensway was built on this site in 1952, and is shown in the modern photograph. The two essential elements for brickmaking, clay to make the bricks and furze to provide the fierce heat to fire the kilns, were in ample supply on Horsham Common. There were still three large brickyards within the town in 1914, making stockbricks in a way peculiar to the south-east of England, using clamps instead of kilns. In 1951, the Sussex Brick and Estates Company, which was then operating in Warnham and Southwater, had its headquarters in Horsham. In the 1980s, 250 men were producing a total of $1\frac{1}{2}$ million high quality bricks each week in Warnham, where brick-making is still carried on. The Southwater brickworks was closed when the supplies of clay were exhausted, and the site has now been turned into a country park.

In 1951, Wickersham Road was a small road leading off London Road into Madeira Avenue, to the north of the Carfax. It was named after a blacksmith who worked there earlier in the century, but was originally known as Lloyd's Yard, because James Lloyd, the carrier, had his premises here in the 1840s. He ran a daily stage wagon to London for the transport of heavy goods, until the coming of the railway in 1848. The carriers were systematically organized, with a regulated scale of charges fixed at the Quarter Sessions from the seventeenth century onwards. They continued to operate locally until the twentieth century – in 1898 Horsham still had a network of carriers going to the nearby villages and towns at fixed times on one or more days a week.

Wickersham Road has now disappeared under Albion Way, but Madeira Avenue remains and is an approach road to Parkside, one of the main buildings of the Royal & Sun Alliance development.

In 1951, Park Street was a quiet residential street with just a few shops and businesses. Now it has become part of the main road through the town, since North Street has become Chart Way. It has also been cut in two by Albion Way, and the southern end, beyond Pirie's Place, is now called Park Place. On the left in the modern photograph is the back of one of the Royal & Sun Alliance buildings next to Albion Way. The coming of the Sun Alliance Insurance Company to Horsham in 1964, in line with Government pressure to relocate businesses and offices outside London, came about almost by chance, because of a casual meeting in a lift and a conversation in which Horsham was mentioned. It provided new opportunities for a mainly white-collar work force, at a time when the traditional businesses were dying out, and the prosperity of the town was at stake. Royal & Sun Alliance now employs more than 2,000 people in Horsham.

Chapter 5

Schools and Public Services

In 1951, this building housed Denne Road Girls' School, but it was originally built as the second Collyer's School in 1840. Richard Collyer, a wealthy London mercer, died in 1532, leaving money in his will for a free grammar school to be set up in Horsham, his home town, to educate poor boys. It was the oldest surviving grammar school in Sussex before it became a sixth form college in 1976. The replacement of the original Tudor building in 1840 was due to the efforts of the then headmaster, William Pirie, who revived the school in the nineteenth century, after a long period of decline. Collyer's School moved to Hurst Road in 1892, and this building was a girls' school until it was pulled down in the 1960s. St Mary's Primary School has now been built on the site. The original Collyer's School contained a large schoolroom flanked by houses for the headmaster and usher. It adjoined the house where Sir Bysshe Shelley, grandfather of the poet, died in 1815.

The main building of Collyer's School in Hurst Road – the third school to be built in the name of Richard Collyer in Horsham – has changed little since 1951, though it has been greatly expanded. It is no longer a school but a sixth form college, celebrating its 25th anniversary in 2001. Collyer's School moved to this spacious new site in Hurst Road in 1892, provided by Robert Henry Hurst, when the original site in Denne Road became too cramped. Collyer's School had a number of long-serving headmasters throughout its history, notably James Alleyn from 1567 to 1617, John Nisbet from 1648 to 1684, the Rev. Francis Osgood from 1722 to 1773, and William Pirie who was in office from 1822 to 1868. In 1951, P.A. Tharp was an outstanding and inspirational headmaster who had been at the school since 1926. Many of his pupils still living in Horsham recall him with great esteem. Two of his masters, J.B. Shrewsbury and G.F.W. Hart, served as curators of Horsham Museum.

Tanbridge House was built by a wealthy railway contractor, Sir Thomas Oliver, in 1887, and was one of the first houses in Horsham to be lit by electricity, produced by its own generator. The site has a long history – it was known as Cadmans in 1427, and the Pancras family, who were tanners, lived there during the sixteenth century. Tanbridge House replaced an older house which was probably built by Richard Nye around 1627. After the death of Sir Thomas Oliver in 1920, Tanbridge House was bought by West Sussex County Council for £7,000, and in 1951 it was the home of Horsham High School for Girls. In 1976, Tanbridge School was established as a comprehensive secondary school for boys and girls, using this building and another where Sainsbury's supermarket now stands. It moved to a new purpose-built site on Farthings Hill, off Guildford Road, in the early 1990s. Tanbridge House has now been converted into apartments, and other houses built in the grounds, in a housing development scheme.

In 1951 the foundations were being laid for Forest School, a secondary modern school for boys in Compton's Lane, on the land of Smithsbarn Farm. This is now the Forest Community School, which houses a boys' secondary school and an adult education centre. Nearby in Depot Road is Millais, now a secondary school for girls but originally the girls' and junior section of Forest School. This part of Horsham was developed during the 1950s as part of a major expansion on the eastern side of the town. The reorganisation of the schools took place when the comprehensive system was adopted in 1976 to cover all secondary education. Horsham's schools have generally performed well in the latest assessment tests, but there is now a growing pressure on places, as the town's population has increased to over 30,000, and the houses now extend up to the northern bypass. Families with young children predominate in the fast-growing civil parish of North Horsham.

The old School of Arts and Crafts in Hurst Road, built in 1891, was started on the initiative of a group of local people in 1881. Miss Edith Harms was one of the outstanding tutors at the school in its early days, and by 1886 the success of her students allowed the school to apply for a grant towards a permanent building. Miss Maud Hurst, an artist herself, trained in Paris, served on the committee which worked hard to raise funds for the school, and her father, Robert Henry Hurst, gave the land. W.H. Bernard Lintott was associated with the school from the start, and finally retired as Chairman of the committee in 1950. The Art School is an attractive building with large windows, ideal for its original purpose. It was built by James Potter, a local builder. But by 1949 the school had outgrown these premises, and had moved to Oakfield, also in Hurst Road. The old school is now the headquarters of the local Womens' Voluntary Services.

The tall chimney of the Council's Electric Works in Stanley Street was still a prominent feature of the Horsham skyline in 1951, seen here behind the Waterworks. Although gas lighting was installed in Horsham in 1836, public services as a whole were slow to develop because Horsham residents, fearing the cost, refused to adopt Public Health Acts until forced to do so in 1872. A private waterworks company was set up in 1865 to supply piped water, but the lack of a sewage system meant that Horsham had a high death rate from enteric fevers, until the Local Board of Health finally installed proper drainage in 1879. Electricity was brought to the town in 1902 by the newly created Horsham Urban District Council. The Electric Works was the first in the country to use recycled household waste. In the modern photograph, the building on the corner of Victoria Street, now the headquarters of St John's Ambulance Brigade, is seen from the west rather than the south.

In 1951, the Fire Station was in Horsham Park, beside Park House, but the new station, shown in the modern photograph, was built in Hurst Road in 1968. Horsham's first fire engine – basically a water cart – was presented to the town before 1724. In 1840, the Horsham Volunteer Fire Brigade was set up, and was supported by the townspeople who subscribed small sums on a regular basis. By 1874, under their captain, Thomas Honywood, the volunteer fire brigade was an enthusiastic and well-trained body of men, but as they had to borrow horses every time they needed to go to a fire, their response time was often rather slow! In 1882, the first proper fire station was built at No. 22 North Street; this housed two engines and had a gallows-like pole at the back for drying the hoses. One of these engines can now be seen in Horsham Museum. A splendid new steam-powered engine was acquired in 1908. West Sussex Fire Brigade took over the local service in 1947.

The police station in Barttelot Road was opened in 1894 and had two cell blocks, the ground floor block for men, and the upstairs block for women, with a central warders' room. This was used as an Armed Forces recruiting office during the First World War. From 1910 to 1922 it was the force headquarters of the West Sussex Constabulary and, for a time during this period, it included the residence of the Chief Constable, Mr Drummond. Because of this, it had a distinctive (and apparently unique) red lamp above its main entrance which indicated its status. In 1949 the Barttelot Road police station was the headquarters of one of the most famous murder enquiries of the last century – the 'acid bath murders' committed by John George Haigh. Haigh was housed in the cells at Barttelot Road when he was arrested, before he appeared before the magistrates in Horsham Town Hall. Horsham police station is now in Hurst Road and the old station has been converted to other uses.

The Horsham Hospital in Hurst Road has expanded considerably since 1951, though it looks little changed in the modern photograph. Horsham people responded generously to an appeal to build a cottage hospital in 1890, and the hospital was built within two years at a cost of £1,950, on land given by Robert Henry Hurst. This larger hospital was built nearby in the 1920s, and greatly extended in the 1980s. Recently, a further extension was built to house out-patient services. The wards are now used mainly for geriatric patients. Under various National Health Service reorganisations, the casualty department and the maternity ward were moved to Crawley, and now maternity services have been moved to the East Surrey Hospital at Redhill, which has caused much local concern. It is very much hoped that a new general hospital will be built at Pease Pottage within the next few years, to restore a comprehensive local medical service for people living in the Horsham and Crawley area.

In 1951 the new Horsham ambulance was proudly displayed outside the St John's Ambulance brigade headquarters in Park Street, by its Commander, Mr Alfred Cottingham, who had a furniture removal business in Worthing Road. At this time the service was still run on a voluntary part-time basis – the lady in the photograph worked at Timothy Whites. The ambulance service became the responsibility of West Sussex County Council in 1963, and now the Sussex Ambulance Service is run by the National Health Service. The ambulance station is now in Hurst Road, along with the police station, the fire brigade, Horsham Hospital, the Royal Mail sorting office and the new court house. This centralisation of all the main public services, with the Horsham District Council offices just round the corner in North Street, makes Horsham a convenient and well-planned small town. The modern photograph of the same site shows part of the Royal & Sun Alliance development, next to the old burgage house called the George, or Botting's.

Chapter 6

Sport, Leisure and Entertainment

This photograph shows the Boxing Day meet of the Crawley and Horsham Hunt, which was held every year in the Carfax, and was a colourful occasion. The hunt no longer meets there, since the rise of the anti-hunting lobby and the Carfax redevelopment. Sussex has long associations with hunting – the famous Charlton and Goodwood hunts were of great social importance in the eighteenth century. The Crawley and Horsham Hunt was operating by 1847, when Mr Lee Steere, who lived in Ockley, joined it with his pack of hounds. The heyday of the Crawley and Horsham Hunt was between 1885 and 1914, when Colonel C.B. Godman was Master. During the Second World War, Mrs Molly Gregson of Ends Place in Warnham took over as Master, and became renowned as a hound breeder and friend of the farming community. A local general practitioner, Dr Geoffrey Sparrow, was an enthusiastic follower of the hunt, and was well-known for his humorous pictures of hunting and huntsmen, now on display at Horsham Museum.

The cricket field, which lies south of St Mary's church, across the River Arun, is little changed from 1951. It was previously known as the Barrack Fields, because it was part of the land leased from Nathaniel Tredcroft from 1796 to 1815, for the building of a barracks in Worthing Road. Edward Tredcroft, a passionate cricketer who played for the Zingari club, gave the ground to Horsham Cricket Club in 1850, and it was bought by Horsham District Council in 1989 to prevent it being sold for redevelopment. Cricket has been played at Horsham since 1768 – John Baker was an enthusiastic spectator of several matches and said in August 1773 that the Horsham cricketers came home in triumph after beating East Grinstead and, 'Horsham boys beat Warnham boys out of sight'. Sussex Cricket Week, when the county side comes to play in Horsham, is still held each year, but in 1951 this was a rather more important occasion in the life of the town than it is today.

The bandstand was moved a few yards during the redevelopment of the Carfax, but the main difference here is that the 1951 photograph was taken looking north and the modern one east. It was built by public subscription in 1892, for performances by local bands or musical groups. Horsham boasted a town band from the early nineteenth century, which became the Royal British Legion Concert Band. William Albery, the saddler who was also Horsham's local historian, co-founded the Horsham Recreation Silver Band in 1900. This band competed in the top division of the Brass Band Championships and made radio broadcasts; later it was known as the Horsham Borough Band, and now its music can be heard on an Internet site. Albery himself played the cornet, and won the Southern Counties Championship. His playing was recorded on an early wax cylinder for the Edison Bell phonograph. The bandstand was restored to its original condition when it was relocated in 1989, and now various local bands can be seen performing here.

Park House (seen here from the rear) was built in 1720 by John Wicker, a brewer who had amassed considerable wealth. It contained a room decorated with exquisite Chinese wallpaper, called the Bird Room. The diarist John Baker leased Park House in 1771 and lived there until 1777. He described a great turtle dinner he gave here, for his friends among the Horsham gentry. Robert Hurst, the lawyer and MP, bought Park House in 1799, and lived here until his death in 1843. He became Horsham's biggest landowner after the enclosure of Horsham Common in 1812. Park House remained in the hands of the Hurst family until 1929, when it was sold to Horsham Urban District Council, and turned into offices. In the foreground of the modern photograph can be seen the award-winning garden specially designed for the blind and disabled, by Sun Alliance and Horsham District Council which was opened in 1991. It contains pieces of masonry from St Mark's church, and a sundial designed by John Skelton, a local artist.

The 1951 photograph of Horsham Park shows the bandstand and open-air swimming pool, which was built by Horsham Urban District Council in 1933 as a job-creation scheme. By 1951, there were also tennis courts and a putting green. Horsham Park was given to the town by the Hurst family after the First World War. When John Baker lived at Park House in the 1770s, the grounds were useful rather than ornamental – he cut the hay in the Great Meadow, and dragged the pond for fish. The Hursts created attractive gardens around the house, but some parts were still cultivated as fields even in 1951. Now the park boasts a Millennium Maze, which contains a sculpture of the St Leonard's Forest Dragon. A new bandstand stands beside an attractive conservatory café, and a much larger covered swimming pool is being rebuilt off Hurst Road. Open-air concerts are given during the summer, and the former Park Recreation Centre has been converted into a ten-pin bowling alley and nightclub.

The 1951 photograph of an old building in Glynde Place shows that it was then the storehouse of Attwater's sports shop in Market Square. It is now a dance studio, which offers classes in ballet and modern dance. In the eighteenth century this building served as a slaughterhouse for the butcher Stringer Sheppard, whose premises fronted Market Square and included the old Half Moon Inn, which later became Attwater's shop. The Sheppards were butchers in Horsham from 1728 to about 1855. When the new floor was laid for the dance studio, the floor of the old slaughterhouse was uncovered and the drainage channels, which clearly revealed their original purpose, were found. This revelation suggests a connection with the brutal sport of bull-baiting which used to take place in Horsham before 1813 – the bull was tethered in a ring marked on the west side of the Carfax and attacked by dogs. The meat from the slaughtered bulls was sold by the local butchers and was said to be especially tender – it seems very likely that Stringer Sheppard's slaughter house was put to use on such occasions. Another Horsham 'sport' of this time was that of wife-selling – but this was a cheap form of divorce for the poor who could not afford lawyers' fees. In the nineteenth century, Bonfire Night provided much entertainment with processions and fireworks – once the bonfire was so large that it scorched houses in the Carfax.

The 1951 photograph shows the Odeon cinema in North Street, from the north-east corner of the Carfax. The Odeon cinema had a distinctive 'lighthouse' outside to advertise its programme. Before this cinema was built in the 1930s, Dr Geoffrey Sparrow and his family lived on this site in a large old house which he said had 'a beautiful old-world garden'. Nearby was the older Winter Garden cinema, which was used by Canadian soldiers stationed in Horsham during the Second World War. While the Odeon 'lighthouse' has disappeared in the extensive redevelopment of this area since 1951, a new 'lighthouse' may be said to have been created in St Mark's Court, the most visible part of the Royal & Sun Alliance development. It is a spectacular glass-walled atrium which soars above Albion Way, and it houses an enormous chandelier of 4,000 pieces,

made in Austria, and weighing one and a half tonnes. This is a very striking feature when seen from the road below, especially at night. The windows of St Mark's Court are etched with views from the Downs Way, the footpath linking the North and South Downs, which passes near Horsham. This is one of several beautiful walks in and around Horsham. The Horsham Society has promoted the creation of a Riverside Walk which encircles the town, and now the High Weald Landscape Trail has been laid out from Horsham to East Grinstead.

In the 1951 view of North Street, looking towards the station, little can be seen except trees and the wall of Horsham Park to the left, but there were two cinemas and the County Library along this road, and many Council offices. The modern photograph shows attractive flowerbeds and trees screening new office blocks on the right. Horsham Arts Centre, to the right of the picture, is now Horsham's main place of entertainment. It contains the Capitol theatre and the Ritz cinema, a studio and an art gallery. The building was originally the Ritz cinema, built in the Art Deco style of the 1930s. The theatre was named after the well-loved Capitol theatre in the Carfax, demolished in 1982 when Swan Walk was extended. There is a long history of theatre in Horsham; companies of strolling players visited the town in the eighteenth century, and there was a theatre here in 1800. A young ensign fell in love with one of the actresses and tried unsuccessfully to shoot her older lover!

Chapter 7

Memories of the Past and People of Horsham

Warnham mill, seen here in 1951, is the oldest remaining mill in Horsham, built in the seventeenth century on two ponds which had originally been used to power the Warnham iron furnace. This furnace was known to have produced cannon for the King's army in the Civil War and was destroyed by Parliamentary troops in 1644. The Shelley family owned the ponds in 1771, and the mill was bought by Timothy Shelley, father of the poet, in 1791. Percy Bysshe is reputed to have learnt how to sail here, and to have written some of his early poems while sitting under a tree near the mill. His first known letter proposes 'a day at the pond' and a picnic to his cousin, Thomas Medwin, who later recalled that the two of them went trout fishing and shooting there as young men. Later, the mill and the ponds were bought by the Lucas family, of Warnham, who restored the mill in 1985. The ponds are now part of Warnham Nature Reserve.

This view of St Mary's church from the cricket ground is little changed from 1951, except for the growth of the trees. The house in the foreground was occupied in 1841 by Daniel Dewdney, bailiff of the Tredcroft estates. This area has been known as the Barrack Fields since the Napoleonic Wars, when Horsham was required to house a large barracks. Twelve acres of land was rented from Nathaniel Tredcroft in 1796, and eight barrack blocks, each holding 120 men, were quickly built near Worthing Road, together with cookhouses, a hospital, mortuary and guardhouse, stables for the cavalry and a parade ground. Thousands of soldiers passed through Horsham, as regiments were quartered in the town for three months or more, until the war ended in 1815. The Rifle Brigade was set up at Horsham in 1800, to train sharp-shooters, who proved their worth at the Battle of Waterloo. The barracks added to the prosperity of the town, but drunken soldiers were sometimes a menace to the repose of the townspeople!

These views of Flagstones, an old house in the Causeway, are taken from the churchyard which it overlooks. It is certainly older than the date given on the front, of 1615, but at that time it belonged to the Church and was the home of the parish clerk, Thomas Foreman. Later it was owned by Stephen Osmer, a glover, and divided into several cottages. In 1805, one of the tenants was Samuel West, a Quaker, who wrote a poem entitled *Reflections among the Tombs in Horsham churchyard*. He was related to Howard Dudley who wrote, printed and engraved the first history of Horsham in 1836, at the age of sixteen. The flat-topped tomb of Helena Bennett can be seen in front of the house in the modern photograph. This is the Anglicised name of a high-born Muslim lady who married a French adventurer, Benoît de Boigne, in India in 1788. He brought her to England but later divorced her, and she died in Horsham in 1853. She was buried facing towards Mecca.

North Chapel, an old building in North Street, near the station, was owned in 1545 by the Brotherhood of St John and St Anne. This religious fraternity was founded in 1457, and its patrons included Thomas Hoo, then MP for Horsham, whose monument can be seen in St Mary's church. Additions were made to the original building in the seventeenth century. North Chapel was divided into three cottages when it was owned by Miss Elizabeth Gatford, a wealthy and eccentric lady, who lived in the Carfax and died in 1799. She kept a wide variety of animals and birds at her home, and provided for their care in her will. She also left money to provide bread for the poor, which was distributed every Sunday at the old Baptist Chapel in Worthing Road. According to her specific instructions, she was not buried until a month after her death, and her body was placed within four coffins, one inside the other. North Chapel has now become an architect's office.

Pump Alley is one of the narrow alleys or 'twittens' which are a feature of Horsham. In this case, the alley was a path between two old inns, one called the Talbot or Wonder on the right in the 1951 photograph, and the other called the Green Dragon on the left. Both of them were burgage properties which even by 1611 had been divided into several parts to give the owners more votes. A description of the burgages drawn up for the 1806 election refers to one 'known by the name of the Wonder or Talbot Inn being the great Parlour ... adjoining to the old Starr inn and half the garrets fronting the market-place'. Today this part of the old Talbot Inn houses a Thai restaurant. The building to the left of the arch was the first Post Office in Horsham in 1840 and also the postmaster's house. Apparently he sat behind a shutter which still exists to the left of the archway, and took in or handed out letters.

Collett's Alley is another 'twitten' off the Carfax, leading through to Middle Street. It was named after Jeremiah Collett who had a baker's shop in the 1840s where Wickersham's the hairdresser was in 1951. The Sussex Tea Rooms now occupies this building, with a fish and chip shop behind it in the alley. Collett's shop previously belonged to Charles Champion, who also had a post windmill on Horsham Common, built by his father in 1765. The Champions ran the mill and the bakery as a joint business for many years. Charles Champion was associated with a charity set up in 1804 by Sir Henry Fletcher in memory of his late wife, Catherine, to make a Christmas distribution of beef and bread to the poor of Southwater. The bread was bought from Charles Champion, who himself left £120 in his will to the churchwardens of St Mary's, to provide bread for the poor every Sunday, if they went to church. Champion's mill had unhappy associations in the 1770s, when public executions were carried out on a temporary gallows nearby. John Baker, the diarist, described the execution there of Ambrose Cannon, a smuggler involved in the murder of a dragoon, on 30 August 1773. In 1775 such executions were moved to the Hanging Plat off Brighton Road. Champion's mill was blown down in a gale in February 1860, when Peter Dale the miller was killed, and his son severely injured.

No. 1 Park Terrace West was on the site of the last Horsham Gaol, built in the part of East Street renamed Queen Street in honour of Queen Victoria. After the Old Gaol in the Carfax was condemned by John Howard in 1774, the Duke of Richmond actively promoted the building of a new 'model' gaol, which was built between 1775 and 1779 by two local carpenters, Thomas and Edward Griffiths, and Ralph Joanes, a stone mason and bricklayer. It was the first gaol in the world to have individual cells for prisoners. There was separate accommodation for men and women, and criminals and debtors. In 1822, a new gallows, nicknamed the 'Horsham Drop', was erected outside the gaol, and public executions were celebrated with Hanging Fairs promoted by the local beershop owners, until the last execution in 1844. After the gaol was pulled down in 1845, Park Square was built on the site. When the railway was extended south in 1859, it cut through the square, and the two sides were later renamed Park Terrace West and Park Terrace East. As Queen Street had to be lowered to go under the railway bridge, this corner house was built with large cellars beneath it, to bring it up to the level of the rest of the terrace. In 1951, the cellars housed Gilling's fish shop.

This stretch of Depot Road in 1951 gives an idea of how Horsham Common was developed after its enclosure in 1812, when it was necessary to make more productive use of the land. Large farms were established which used better farming methods, and long straight roads were built across it. In 1951 this area was still not built up, and the land on the left was used as allotments. Now Millais School is on the right of the modern picture. Millais School was named after J.G. Millais, the son of the painter, who lived nearby at Compton's Brow, a large house which was demolished in the 1960s when Harwood Road was built as a relief road for Roffey. J.G. Millais wrote a major scholarly work on the mammals of Great Britain, and a book on magnolias, which he collected and grew in his Horsham garden. He was also a talented artist and sculptor, and his bronze of two fighting cocks can be seen in the garden of Horsham Museum.

This part of Queen Street, seen from the end of Park Terrace East, was just about to be rebuilt in 1951. On the left was the Alexandra public house, now an office but still with the rose emblem sign on the wall. The modern terrace of shops next to the railway bridge replaced the nineteenth-century houses and shops, which were demolished before the Second World War, when the nearby brickyard was abandoned. In the distance were the old Town Fields, scene of a bitter dispute between Pilfold Medwin and Lady Shelley, mother of Percy Bysshe, in the 1840s. The fields had belonged to the Medwins but had been sold to Sir Timothy Shelley in 1829 with the understanding that he would provide his cousin Mary Medwin, the widow of Thomas Charles, with an annuity for the rest of her life. When Sir Timothy Shelley died in 1844, Lady Shelley claimed a large sum in back rent, through her agent Dewdney Stedman, which deeply upset Pilfold.

In 1951 these old cottages in London Road, on the opposite side of the road to the rather grander Brunswick Place and Sussex Terrace, were a surviving part of an earlier Horsham. The small cottages were the houses of a number of small tradesmen and traditional craftsmen – there was still a wheelwright and blacksmith's shop, which has now been re-erected at Amberley Industrial Museum, and a bootmaker and chimney-sweep. One of the cottages was previously a public house called The Good Intent. Now the old building on the right, known as Mr Mill's cottages, has been replaced by Jasmine Court, which provides sheltered housing. In 1841, one of the most loveable Horsham 'characters' described by Henry Burstow lived in this part of London Road. Isaac Aldridge was a carpenter by trade, but he was also the organ-blower and chief bell-ringer at St Mary's church, looked after the fire engine, and wielded his drumsticks with extraordinary flourishes as the big drummer of the Town Band!

This area, which used to be called Grub Street, and is now Highlands Road, lies to the east of the station and suffered during the Second World War, when several people were killed and eight houses destroyed by three high explosive bombs dropped on 29 November 1940. It was one of the areas first developed on Horsham Common in the nineteenth century – a group of broom and basket makers lived there in 1841. There has been speculation as to how Grub Street got its name, which was in general usage until the 1930s. Probably the town's rubbish dumps were here at one time, and people used to come and grub around in them. It has been thought that there might possibly be some connection with the Grub Street writers of eighteenth century literary London – the hack journalists attacked by Alexander Pope – as Pope's works were published by the printer Bernard Lintot, who came from Horsham. But this theory seems to be somewhat far-fetched.

The large building on the right in the 1951 photograph was built in Park Street in 1873 by Capt. Egerton Hubbard as the headquarters and drill hall of the Horsham company of Volunteers, formed after the Crimean War and called the 7th Sussex Volunteer Corps. These amateur soldiers were the pride of the town, and were well accommodated, trained and disciplined. In 1908, the 4th Battalion of the Royal Sussex Regiment was formed out of the Volunteers as a reserve, but in 1914 it was quickly reorganized on a war footing. Horsham soldiers served in Gallipoli, Egypt, Palestine and on the Western Front during the First World War. In 1951, the building was being used by Durtnalls as a furniture depository. The Park Hotel in the background was owned by Mr W.A.E. Marsh, whose grand-daughter now runs it as an antiques centre. The multi-storey car park built as part of the Pirie's Place shopping centre in 1990 has now replaced all the other buildings shown in 1951.

In 1951, this cottage in Rusham's Road was next door to a doll's hospital, owned by Mr Ellison, which can be seen on the right. The Kipps family who lived there had moved down from London some eighteen months earlier. The little girl sitting on the step to the left was Carole Kipps, then aged three, with her mother and sister Jackie to the right. The photograph was taken by their father Reg Kipps, then a member of the Horsham Photographic Society. The site is now a petrol station and the cottage has disappeared. This part of the town, bounded by the north end of Rusham's Road, Trafalgar Road, Kempshott Road and Spencer's Road, was known as The Common. It was largely built up in the nineteenth century and had a very definite sense of identity in 1951, plus a strong community spirit. The south end of Rusham's Road and the surrounding area was built up by the Davis building company of Croydon in the 1930s.

This is a very evocative photograph of three young girls walking through Pump Alley in 1951 – almost certainly in the early morning, because the sunlight is low and coming from the east. They were probably on their way to church or to school as they are all smartly dressed. It vividly recalls the Horsham of 1951, but the girls seem to be striding confidently into the future. The modern photograph shows the 'greening' of Horsham which has taken place in recent years, as well as some updating of the buildings. Great efforts have been made to beautify the town in order that Horsham should do well in various Britain in Bloom competitions, and several good results have been achieved. A historic old town, whose centre has been skilfully redeveloped, much high quality new housing, an active community spirit and a diversified economy, have all contributed to making Horsham a good place to live at the beginning of the twenty-first century.